Twenty Tips for Teaching IGCSE ESL

by

Dr Rosemary Westwell

CONTENTS   PAGE

WORKSHEETS (suggested answers may be found on page 51)

INTRODUCTION

'Tips for Teaching IGCSE English as a Second Language' offers student-centred exercises for improving speaking, listening, reading, writing and grammar. Teachers are reminded of quick and easy ways to raise their students' level of achievement.

The author, Dr Rosemary Westwell taught English as a Foreign Language for over 20 years. As Head of EFL in an English public school, there was limited time to improve the end-of-year examination prospects for her students. The ideas and suggestions offered in this workshop arose from her experiences with these classes. Many of the exercises and ideas are also included in the author's book 'Teaching Language Learners' but most are adapted for the level required for this type of examination.

Examinations for students who have English as a Second Language generally expect students to have a working knowledge of English that needs refining for the examination. The exercises are targeted at the advanced members of the class, but are easily adapted to those who are less able.

The big question: Given constraints on scheduling and time, how can we encourage our examination students to learn quickly and effectively?
The simple answer is to devise methods that accelerate the process of language acquisition:

TIP 1: BE GUIDED BY THE PROCESS OF LANGUAGE ACQUISITION

It is commonly accepted that students learn language by:

a. 'noticing' elements of the target language,

b. relating these elements to their previously acquired language and

c. absorbing the new language as part of their current language knowledge through use.

These principles underlie the accompanying worksheets e.g.

    a. tasks engage students with particular aspects of the language

    b. students are encouraged to personalise the language and then

    c. students practise using the newly acquired language a number of times after which

    d. students are encouraged to recall what they have learnt in different ways over gradually increasing periods of time.

Never *tell* your students anything, always *ask* questions first — even of yourself. For example:

Question 1. How can we get our students to focus on satisfying the requirements of the examination?

A suggested 'answer': Get students to 'notice' examination requirements and to relate to them on a personal level by asking them which requirements they need the most help with, e.g., teach the vocabulary in **worksheet 1 (What do you need most?)** by asking the students questions such as 'Which words do you not understand?' Then ask other students to try to explain the meanings. When all the terms are understood, ask the students to complete the worksheet as individuals.

Question 2: How can we persuade our students to engage with these requirements in ways that will raise their level of achievement quickly?
A suggested 'answer': Put the onus onto the students to do the most work, for example:

a. Use errors from the students' written work as the subject of your following lessons e.g. list examples of errors from each piece of writing for the class to try to correct or improve. When they have exhausted their ideas, provide them with the answers

b. Use the examples of **answers to Worksheet 2** to introduce the notions of register and style. (Initial familiarity makes a more thorough approach later more effective).

c. Use **Worksheet 3 (Can you correct these errors?) and 4 (Can you correct these common errors?)** as a basis for revision or for adding one or two more examples that you plan to teach in the near future.

d. When providing corrections, ask the students why the example is incorrect. Extend the questions to other, related issues. For example, if there is a missing article, (as in 'My father is manager') ask when articles are used and when they are not used. (A simplified explanation could be: 'a' is used when we do not know the specific thing or person as in 'Does the company have a manager?', 'the' is used when we do know which thing or person as in 'The manager of the company is away.' and no article is used if the noun is uncountable (such as 'money'), as in 'Money is at the heart of most problems in business'. Follow this with team games in which students try to use given nouns with and without articles.

e. create worksheets that encourage students to teach each other e.g. **worksheet 25**. In pairs, student A has 'the answers' to the first part of the material, student B the answers to the second part. Student B tries to complete the gap fill in the first section. Student A gives hints until student B guesses correctly. They swap roles for the second half of the material.

TIP 3: TEACH *THE STUDENTS* NOT THE SUBJECT: STUDENT ASSESSMENT

Assess the students' current level by asking them to write about themselves and their competency in English e.g., **Worksheet 2 (introduce yourself: writing)**

a. Use the completed examples of worksheet 1 to 'assess' the current level of ability in the students. Teach to the top of the class but maintain awareness of the needs of the less able in the class.

b. Use the errors made in the students' answers as a guide for additional questions to revisit areas of difficulty in short quizzes as the end of lessons to revise the main content of the lesson.

c. Ask the class to discuss the topics most of the class is interested in: for example, sport, music, food … Follow this by asking them to provide 5 words or phrases that are relatively new to them and that they think they will find useful. Encourage them to use the Internet or their current textbook as resources. If time is very limited, you could provide a list from which students select the examples they think would be most useful.

d. Encourage students to use these new words in exercises that concentrate on something else, such as nouns and the use of articles. (Killing two birds with one stone in this way speeds up the learning process.)

e. Ask other students to 'mark' the work of their peers but make sure you check their 'marking' has been valid.

f. Encourage students to speak in threes so that 2 of the students can hold a conversation or interview, while the third students tries to notice errors and comments afterwards on the effectiveness of the speakers.

g. Play games such as giving each group of students a die to throw. The students with the highest score speaks for half a minute on a topic chosen by the students, or uses an example of contained in the previous work of the lesson.

h. Ask students to remind the class what they have learnt in the lesson and what they learned in previous lessons.

i. After eliciting information from the class ask a student/team to summarize what has just been 'discovered'.

TIP 4: MAKE LEARNING APPEAR QUICK AND EASY: VOCABULARY

Introduction

It is believed that language is stored in the memory according to the sound and meaning of the words. Using this knowledge, students can be encouraged to learn vocabulary quickly and more permanently by focusing on the sounds and meaning of the separate words.

Example: Work

There are a number of associated words students should know: e.g.,
employer, the boss, the director, the managing director, the chief of staff, a public relations officer, bursar, accountant, clerk, administrative clerk, staff, colleagues …
architect, librarian, engineer, nurse, doctor, surgeon, policeman/woman, plumber, electrician, driver, computer programmer, mechanic, shop assistant, factory worker, artist, musician …
office, library, hospital, factory, office, study, garage, pub, hotel, surgery, department store, supermarket …
answer an advertisement, apply for a job, go for an interview, accept a position, to take leave, a leave of absence, to resign, to retire, …

Take a single group of similar-sounding words, extend the students' knowledge of these words and encourage them to use these immediately afterwards e.g.

Work: elicit more words and/or phrases related to 'work'

e.g., draw up a chart for students to complete:

noun work, workbench, workaholic, workmate, work regime, work station …

adjective overworked, underworked, working, workable, unworkable

verb to work, to overwork,

associated pronouns/phrases/or clauses: to work over the detail; to work within the remit/parameters; to be in work; to work for someone; to work through a problem; to work under someone; to work over someone; to work on a proposal; to work at home; to work in the office; to work away from home; to work yourself into a sweat/corner …

After drawing up a similar chart, students will learn the vocabulary easily if encouraged to talk about how these words are or to relate them to their own or others' experiences. Follow this with a written exercise and the words should soon become part of the students' working vocabulary.

Draft follow up exercises such as **worksheet 5**

TIP 5: DON'T 'TEACH' GRAMMAR, PLAY WITH IT: PARTS OF SPEECH

Ask the students what they know already, and then provide a 'fool proof' worksheet for them to discover what you need to teach. For example, **worksheet 6 Name the part of speech**

Then quiz them further, in team games or as a class quiz, introducing 'new' terms one at a time. for example, write 'thought' and 'apple' on the board and ask which is an 'abstract' noun and which is a 'concrete' noun and why. Ask them for more examples. Allow the students to wander off the topic such as talking about the qualities of concrete. This way they will remember something positive from the lesson because they have contributed to it.

Information to play with:

Nouns:

Abstract nouns: *thought, idea, hope, anger ...*

Concrete nouns: *apple, book, coat ...*

Compound nouns: *housecoat, bedroom, courthouse, foghorn, guildhall, pothole, greenhouse, hothouse, lighthouse, jailbird, carport, manhole, pillbox, hatbox, motorcar, earring, facelift, hairnet, beeswax, netball handball, football, backpack, kneepad, dustpan, hatpin, hairpin, anthill, molehill, sandpit, quarterdeck, yardstick, website, armrest, chinrest, ribcage, windowsill ...*

Synonyms *finger + digit; wonderful + marvellous; bad + evil; sad + unhappy ...*

Antonyms *black - white; good - bad; right - wrong; right - left ...*

Verbs: of action: *walk, run, skip, jump ...*

auxiliary verbs: *'be' e.g. I am walking; 'do' e.g. They do not work.; 'have' e.g. I have come.*

modal verbs: *can, could, may might, shall, should will, would, must, ought to, used to, need, had better and dare*

Adverbs: *quickly, slowly, leisurely ...; recently, lately, often, seldom, never, hardly ever, always ...*

Adjectives: *red, orange, yellow, green, blue ...; large, small, wide, deep, thick, thin ...; bad, good, marvellous, wonderful ...; wooden, plastic, nylon ...; English, French, Italian, Spanish ...; old, young, middle-aged ...;*

Prepositions: *to, away, from, at, over, near, under, by, opposite, next to, of, off ...*

Conjunctions: *and, but*

Articles (a, the) and determiners: *a, the, these, those ...*

Interjections: *Oh! Oh dear! Help! Oops!*

TIP 6: GIVE THE STUDENTS A HANDLE ON THE TENSES

Worksheets 7 and 8 encourage the students to 'notice' the verb tenses. Follow these by activities that encourage the students to **use** the different verb tenses, for example:

Present simple:

- In pairs, students describe their daily or weekly routine.

Present continuous

- The teacher and then students mime an action. Remaining students say what the teacher or student is doing.

Past simple

- In pairs students describe what they did yesterday/last week/for their last holiday …

Past continuous

- Students describe the weather yesterday.

Future

Will: Students study each other's palms and predict futures.

Going to: Students provide 3 statements saying what they are going to do after school/next week/next weekend. One statement is a lie. The other students guess which statement is not true.

Present perfect

- In pairs, students ask each other 'Have you ever …?' e.g. won a prize/forgotten a friend's birthday/been on a plane … Students compile their own list of questions and answers.

Present perfect continuous

- Students describe how long they have been learning English/ texting on a mobile phone/ /attending this school … Students compile their own list of suggestions to continue.

Past perfect

- Students provide dramatic statements in the past e.g. the car crashed/the boat sank/the tree crashed to the ground. Then ask the students what had happened to cause the event e.g. the driver had fallen asleep/a storm had suddenly appeared/ lightning had struck the tree ... Students compile their own list of suggestions to continue.

Past perfect continuous

- Students describe what they had been doing before they came to school, what their friends/parents/had been doing before they had gone to work

TIP 7: GET THE STUDENTS TO CORRECT THEIR OWN MISTAKES

Introduce the students to an editing guide such as the one in **Worksheet 9** by asking them to complete an accompanying worksheet.

From then on, use the Editing Guide to mark the students' work so that they correct their own mistakes.

For example, if they have written the following sentence:

'I is student. I always go to home late in Wednsdays.'

Underline there the errors have occurred and number them according to the descriptions provided by **Worksheet 9 The Editing Guide**

For example:

   2   1   10   5   6

'I is student. I always go to home late in Wednsdays.'

Students write their corrections next to the errors and all you need to do is to check they have corrected their work successfully. The Editing Guide serves a dual purpose: not only do students notice and correct their errors, by reading and rereading the Guide they are being taught the grammar they need as an individual.

Follow this with activities that encourage the students to **notice, relate** and **use** and the correct grammar when writing:

- Students write an essay or story. Students swap essays or stories and underline possible errors. Possible errors are written on the board for students in teams to accept, try to correct or improve. Successful corrections or improvements are given points by the teacher.

- The teacher collects errors from the students' written work. The errors are written on the board for teams to try to correct or improve.

- The Teacher divides the class into two teams. The teacher then presents a quiz on common errors for the teams to take it in turn to correct the errors. Each correct answer scores a point.

- The teacher collects students' errors that have been corrected by the class over the week/month and prepares a short written test in which the students recall how to correct the errors.

TIP 8: MAKE PRONUNCIATION PLAY

Provide students with a pronunciation chart such as **worksheet 11**.

Devise a worksheet that will encourage the students to notice the contents of the pronunciation chart such as **worksheet 12**.

Then devise activities that encourage the students to relate to, use and recall correct pronunciation

- The teacher explains a pronunciation chart indicating the sounds the symbols represent. The teacher then divides the class into two teams and gives them a quiz on the content of the chart.

- The teacher listens to the students during their speaking activities and lists pronunciation errors. The teacher writes words that contain the sounds the students are finding difficult. The words and their pronunciation are discussed. In teams, students provide other words that sound similar.

- The teacher selects pair sounds for the students to practice e.g. the vowel sounds in reed and red. Students provide similar sounding words from clues given by the teacher. e.g. Today I am reading a book. Yesterday I ….. a different book. (answer read). Students write the words on the board to 'notice' the spelling.

- The teacher asks the students to provide a sentence or more on a topic. The teacher writes what the students says on the board, spelling the words as they sound e.g., I sink zat iss bed. (The student was trying to say 'I think that is bad'.) The pronunciation is corrected by the student(s) until the sentence is written correctly.

- Extend the exercises to include ways in which words are stressed as individual words and within sentences or questions. Use **worksheet 13**

- Students read a text out loud. The teacher listens to the stress patterns in words they find difficult. These words are then written on the board and general rules, if possible, are elicited from the students e.g. words of 3 or more syllables are usually stressed on the penultimate syllable e.g. pollUtion, communicAtion; prefixes and suffixes e.g. com-, -tion, are not usually stressed …

- Students are given a sentence. The teacher asks the students to locate the most important word in the sentence. Students try to stress that word when saying the sentence out loud. e.g., 'I gave John the PARCEL yesterday.' Students are asked what question the sentence would answer e.g., 'What did you give him yesterday?' Students are asked for the different questions that change the stress pattern of the sentence e.g., 'WHEN did you give John the parcel? I gave John the parcel YESTERDAY.' …

TIP 9: EXPLORE THE DIFFERENCE BETWEEN FACTS, IDEAS AND OPINIONS

Ask students to define the difference between a fact, an idea and an opinion.
(Definitions may be:
A fact is a statement that can be true or false.
An idea is a thought or suggestion relating to a situation
An opinion is a statement of what an individual believes, whether it is backed up by facts or not.)

- Ask the students to provide their own examples of a fact, an idea and an opinion.

- Give each individual student a page from a newspaper. In groups students select a fact, an idea and an opinion to share with the class.

Use **worksheets 14, 15, 16 and 17** for students to 'play' with facts. Student A holds one of the quiz answer sheets. Student A reads out each statement in turn. Student B tries to guess the right answers to complete the statements correctly.
The quizzes are activities that encourage students to '**notice**' facts.
An activity that encourage students to '**relate**' facts to their own knowledge and experience:
- Students select facts from their own past, change some of the details and devise a true/false quizz for others to answer

Activities that encourage students to '**use**' facts:

- Students use the internet to list more facts about a chosen topic. Students devise their own quizzes for others to answer.
- Students prepare to give a 2-minute speech on a subject of their choice. The class is given the subject. The members of the class write down any facts they know about the topic. While the talk is being given students listen for their facts. The one with the most facts repeated 'wins'.
- Students use the internet to list more facts about a chosen topic. Students devise their own true/false quizzes for others to answer.
- Students select facts from a page of newspaper or other text, change some of the facts and devise their own true/false quizzes for others to answer.

Activities that encourage students to '**recall**' facts:
- Students compete to complete the final detail of a given fact, e.g. 'The capital of England is ___' (London)
- In teams, students compete to recall as many facts as they can about a previously given topic.
- In pairs students take it in turns to give as many facts as possible about a topic they know well (e.g. family, home …). The listener tries to remember as many facts as possible and repeats them in the different form e.g. student A There are four people in my family. Student B There are more than three and less than five people in your family.

TIP 10: TAKE RISKS: GET YOUR STUDENTS TO EXPRESS OPINIONS:

- Students add to this list of phrases that are commonly used when people express opinions or they select the words they believe are the most formal and informal:
  I think, I feel, they should/shouldn't, If they didn't, they wouldn't, it's wrong to, I agree, they are in agreement with, we don't see eye to eye, we are of the same mind, they are of the same opinion, I beg to differ, I disagree, they hold a different opinion, we failed to agree, I am at odds with, they clashed with, we support the view that, I have no opinion about ...

- The students provide more examples of statements that are used to emphasize an opinion or the teacher provides such statements with the words out of order. Students reassemble the statements. *e.g. I really believe ... There is no doubt that .... It is an accepted fact that ... Most people do not know that .... Evidence shows that ... Anybody who is at all informed about the subject knows that ...*

- Students practice finishing the above statements, emphasizing the key words.

- Students read a text and use these expressions to express their own opinions about the text and its contents.

- Students add to this list of controversial subjects and in pairs express their opinions about these subjects:
  The state should provide pocket money for everyone. Home work should be banned. All doctors should have to attend communication courses. Everyone should have 9 weeks holiday a year. Mothers should be paid as child carers. Mobile phones, iphones and similar items should be used in class all the time. Schools should run on flexi-time. Public transport should be free. Strikes that affect tourists should be banned. ...

- Students write a letter of complaint stating the facts and their opinions about a particular problem and ask for changes to be made.

- Students add to this list of topics: *Talking, sport, reading, music, films, food, education, shopping, sleeping ...* In pairs, students find out the 10 things that their partner likes and dislikes about these topics.

- After listening to students expressing their opinions on a number of topics, students try to recall the opinions that they agreed and disagreed with

TIP 11: ENCOURAGE STUDENTS TO EXPLORE ORIGINAL IDEAS

- The students revise their understanding of the difference between facts, opinions and ideas by providing examples of statements that indicate whether something is a fact, an opinion or an idea or the teacher provides such statements with words out of order, e.g.
  Fact: 'that is not true … It is a well known fact that … I am sorry, you are misinformed … The newspaper/TV/media state that …
  Opinion: That is only your opinion,   That is only an opinion, it is not based on fact … That is what you think, others think differently
  Idea: You could …, What about the idea of doing..?, How about doing …? Perhaps it could be … ? Students reassemble the statements and work out the stress patterns. Students practise in pairs finishing the statements in conversations, emphasizing the key words.

- Students in turn tell the class a fact about themselves, an opinion they hold/held and an idea they have/had. One of them is false – the class tries to identify which one is false.

- Students write an essay in response to a problem e.g. How can save our planet? Students include facts about our planet and the state of it, opinions they hold and that are held by others and ideas people have suggested that will solve the problem.

- Students compete to remember correctly facts opinions and ideas mentioned in previous lessons.

- Students compete to suggest original activities for the class to do in the future.

- Students compile a list of questions that begin with 'What would you do if? Students in pairs or teams try to answer the questions.

- Using these explanations of 'register' and 'style', ask the students how many different ways could they gain experience in recognizing these differences.

'Register' concerns a particular choice of vocabulary and grammar, by speakers and writers in a particular situation. The most basic difference is described as the use of 'formal' and 'informal' language. 'Formal' language is used in formal situations such as at formal meetings, in academic institutions or when meeting important dignitaries. 'Informal' language is used in informal situations such as in everyday conversations, when meeting friends or within a family.

'Style', on the other hand, not only concerns register but looks at the way the words, sentences and paragraphs are put together. A particular author may have a preferred style – e.g. Jane Austen. 'Style' also concerns the correct or conventional use of language e.g. is ending sentences with prepositions using a correct/appropriate style of English for the purpose intended?

TIP 12: DEVISE EASY WAYS FOR STUDENTS TO REGISTER 'REGISTER'

- Ask the students which definition matches 'register' and which describes 'style':

  This word concerns a particular choice of vocabulary and grammar, by speakers and writers in a particular situation. The most basic difference is described as the use of 'formal' and 'informal' language. 'Formal' language is used in formal situations such as at formal meetings, in academic institutions or when meeting important dignitaries. 'Informal' language is used in informal situations such as in everyday conversations, when meeting friends or within a family. (answer: 'register')

  This word not only concerns choice of vocabulary and grammar, but looks at the way words, sentences and paragraphs are put together. A particular author may have a preferred way of wiring in this manner e.g. Jane Austen. It also concerns the correct or conventional use of language. (answer: 'style')

- Ask students to complete **worksheet 19**

- Students discuss which registers are most important in particular situations. Students and/or the teacher search the internet for examples of the use of these registers. Students assist in drawing a summary of the differences between these registers.

- Students describe their own experiences regarding register and/or style, for example, parents complaining about their use of language.

- Students write a description or a story. Using the thesaurus on their computers, they substitute vocabulary to make their writing more formal or informal.

- Students provide examples of problems e.g. I am too tired to study at night. Students write a letter to a friend complaining about this problem, One of the letters is selected and the class change the letter into a formal letter of complaint.

- In teams, students compete to describe the register of particular words. Then they compete to provide an alternative word in a different named register.

- Students name the register in a verbal or written test.

- Students explore the usage of the word 'register' in other contexts.

- Students revisit the given answers to **worksheet 2** and describe the registers of the given examples.

TIP 13: GIVE THE STUDENTS A SENSE OF STYLE

- After completing **worksheet 20**, students write their own examples of the different styles to give to their partner to correct and name the style.

- Students assist in drawing up a chart that describes the differences between the styles.

- Students search the internet for a site they can recommend that gives a description of different styles of writing.

- Students search the internet for more examples of the different styles of writing.

- In a team game quiz, students match the audience with the appropriate language style: (The examples of different types of audience are written on the board for reference)
Different types of audience: university students reading a thesis, a group of professors, at the headmaster's table, friends, a newspaper editor, readers of classical literature, short story readers, audience to a political speech, a group of children in a lesson at school, poetry lovers. e.g. Academic: university students reading a thesis

1. Academic **<u>university students reading a thesis</u>**

2. Elaborate **<u>a group of professors</u>**

3. Formal **<u>people at the headmaster's table</u>**

4. Informal **<u>friends</u>**

5. Journalistic a **<u>newspaper editor</u>**

6. Literary **<u>readers of classical literature</u>**

7. Narrative **<u>short story readers</u>**

8. Oratorical **<u>audience at a political speech</u>**

9. Plain **<u>a group of children in a lesson at school</u>**

10. Poetic **<u>poetry lovers</u>**

- In pairs students explain a simple procedure. The partner guesses what the procedure is. Partners are exchanged. The procedure is explained again but this time to a specific type of audience e.g. children, adults, technicians, actors …The partner guesses what type of audience is being addressed.

TIP 14: GETTING ATTITUDE: MAKE INFERENCES

Students need to understand the attitude contained within texts. Attitude is not always immediately apparent. Attitude is sometimes determined by making inferences, deductions or conclusions, e.g. 'He walked slowly to the door.' may be an indication that the character is unwilling, reluctant or feels guilty.

Ask the students which descriptions match the meaning of inference, deduction and conclusion?

Something that you believe to be true is drawn from information that you already know, e.g. what have you drawn from the description he gave? It may, or may not be true. (**inference**)

Making a judgement about something based on the information that you already have e.g. He found the guilty person. His powers of _____ were impressive. It is based on stronger evidence and is likely to be true. (**deduction**)

Something you decide after you have considered all the information you have been given, e.g. 'After she had thought about all that he had said to her in the past, she came to the _____ that he would never return.' It is a compilation of true facts in a text so is most likely to be true. (**conclusion**)

- Students provide examples or the teacher provides jumbled examples of inference relating to a given statement
  e.g. statement: The writer copied his work from a magazine/newspaper/book.
  e.g. sentences from which the reader may infer the statement:
  'The writer was not an original thinker.'
  'Some of the readers felt uneasy about the writer's work. It seemed very familiar.'
  'The writer was not always diligent in adapting his resources to make sure his work was original.'

- Students try to give examples of situations in which inferences, deductions and conclusions play or played an important part. e.g., when a student says to someone that they 'look healthy' a response may be 'Are you inferring that I am fat? the methods of Sherlock Holmes (deduction); the final paragraph in an essay (conclusion).

- Students provide example sentences describing an event about the past. The remaining students try to determine the attitude of the students now and at the time of the event, supporting their view(s) from the text.

- Competing teams take it in turn to add a sentence to a class review of a book, play, story or news item they have recently read/seen/heard. The sentences that have the most scope for inferring more information score the highest points e.g. The play was unusual= not easily understood? Too outrageous to be credible? Poorly structured?

TIP 15: SHOW STUDENTS HOW TO TAKE CONTROL OF CONVERSATIONS

- The students provide examples of statements that are used to manage conversations or the teacher provides such statements with words out of order e.g.: e.g. I am sorry to interrupt you, but …, What do you think?, I have spoken enough now. It is your turn, . Students reassemble the statements and work out the stress patterns. In pairs, students practise finishing the statements in conversations.

- In teams, students suggest suitable topics for discussion e.g. past and present schooling, future plans, current affairs … In teams, students list suitable questions to ask relating to a chosen topic. e.g. open-ended questions e.g. not 'How long have you been at school?' but 'How do you think school benefits students?' In pairs, students ask and answer the questions. Groups are changed to 2 or 3 students and the class discusses how to manage group conversations and how to extend conversations. Groups speak further on the topic until the topic is exhausted.

- The students provide examples of statements that are used to ask for clarification in conversations or the teacher provides such statements with words out of order e.g. I am sorry but could you repeat that please? …, I'm sorry but would you remind repeating what you just said? I missed it … Could you say that again please? … Could you expand on what you have just said? I am not sure I fully understand … . Students reassemble the statements and work out the stress patterns. Students practise in pairs responding to the statements in conversations.

- The students provide examples of statements that are used to fill silences in conversation when the speakers believe they have nothing to say or the teacher provides such statements with words out of order e.g. I am sorry I quite lost the thread of what I was saying. Where was I? … Just a moment please. I need to think about this … I am not sure what I can add to what I have already said. What do you think? … Students reassemble the statements and work out the stress patterns. Students practise in pairs using these statements in conversations.

- The students provide examples of statements that are used to continue conversations or the teacher provides such statements with words out of order. In pairs, students try to keep their partner talking by using statements that ask them to continue e.g. Why do you think that? … How do you feel about that? … What else can you say about that? … What you say is very interesting. Please continue …

- Students recall ways in which conversations are managed or typical phrases used when managing conversation mentioned in previous lessons in a verbal or written test.

TIP 16: GET STUDENTS TO HEAR WHAT THEY ARE LISTENING TO

- Students sit in silence in the room. They note any sounds they hear and provide a fact and an idea as well as an opinion about them e.g. birdsong: It is a blackbird singing, It is probably protecting its territory, I like the sound of the blackbird.

- The teacher presents a dialogue or a conversation involving 3 or more people. Students listen for the number and kind of contributors and for the number of facts, ideas or opinions expressed.

- In pairs students prepare dialogues between anonymous speakers. The dialogues are read to the class. The class works out the gender, age and intentions of the speakers.

- The teacher gives students every alternate line of a dialogue. Students try to fill the missing lines. The teacher read the full dialogue to the students.

- Students prepare a list of expected phrases in announcements (on TV, at airports and at bus and railway stations). In pairs students prepare an announcement to read to the class. They also prepare and accompanying quiz about the announcement. The other students guess where the announcement was made and answer the quiz.

- In teams students compete to remember announcements they have heard in the past or in the school. They write a list of announcements they expect to hear in the future. The teacher makes several announcements. Students check their examples to see if any match.

- Students select words from a talk to use in their own unprepared 'talks' to other students.

- Students prepare a talk on a topic of their choice. They present the talk to the class. The class makes notes on the fact, ideas and opinions heard.

- In pairs, students practise speaking for a given time limit on given topics. A listens to B and comments afterwards on the facts, ideas and opinions given. Roles are reversed.

TIP 17: MAKE SPELLING MAGIC

<u>Spelling Guide</u>

A sample of 10 spelling rules:

1. 'i' before 'e' except after 'c' e.g. chief, receipt

2. add 'e' to words with short vowels to change them into long vowels
e.g. short vowels a, e, i, o, u as in 'cap', 'bed', 'it', 'on', 'us' (short vowels)
change to long vowels that sound like: ae, ee, ie, oe, ue as in 'cape', 'been', 'bite', 'bone', 'tune' (long vowels)

3. when adding '-ed':
with long vowels there is one consonant in the middle e.g. 'boned'
with short vowels, the consonant is doubled e.g. 'bannedd'

4. to add '–ing', drop the 'e' e.g. make – making

5. to add 'y' at the end of a word:
   When there are two consonants before, keep the 'e' e.g. 'donkey'.
   When there is one consonant before, drop the 'e' e.g. 'shaky'.

6. double the 'll' when 'full' is alone
   Take away an 'l' when 'ful' is at the end e.g. 'He was full of thanks - he was thankful.'

7.- tion has a vowel before (as in station)
   -sion does not (as in mansion) e.g. nation, pension

8. ante with 'e' means 'before', anti with 'i' means 'against'
e.g. anteroom, antenatal, anticlimax, anticlockwise, antifreeze

9. 'c' with 'k' is 'c' (pronounced 'k') as in 'pack'
   'c' on its own is 'c' (pronounced 's') as in 'pace'

10. -cious, -tious have a vowel before (as in 'precious' and 'cautious')
    -scious does not (as in 'conscious')
e.g. 'vicious', 'cautious', 'audacious'

- Introduce the above spelling rules and in teams, students compete to add words to the spelling guide list.

- Students write a story and exchange it with other students. Students underline possible spelling errors. Errors are written on the board for teams to accept or correct. Students write a paragraph or story including as many of the given words as possible.

- Students in teams compete to compile a list of words spelt similarly e.g. words using 'ea' e.g. bead, bread, dead ... Students write a paragraph or story including as many of the given words as possible. (see examples of homonyns in **worksheet 24**)

TIP 18: MAKE PUNCTUATION EASY

- Students complete **worksheets 21 and 22**

- Using **worksheet 21**, students are given the first example. Teams compete to complete the punctuation chart

- Students write a story, leaving out all punctuation. Students swap stories and try to add punctuation. The original story writer accepts or rejects the suggested punctuation and writes the story out in full with the correct punctuation except for one example. A different student tries to identify the error.

- The teacher dictates a passage leaving the students to enter appropriate punctuation. The teacher provides the correct punctuation.

- Students copy a paragraph from a magazine, leaving out the punctuation. They then try to add the punctuation from memory, finally checking their answers from the original text.

- Students make up sounds that represent some of the punctuation marks. In pairs they read a text sounding out the punctuation as they read.

- Students make up sounds that represent some of the punctuation marks. In pairs students A reads a text and pauses before a punctuation mark. Student B makes the sound of the expected punctuation mark or simply gives its name.

- Advanced students compete in teams to provide examples that are seriously affected when the wrong punctuation is used or e.g. The tri-athlete rides runs, and swims. (The tri-athlete rides, runs and swims.)

- Students read examples of blank verse and change the meaning of the poem by altering the punctuation.

- In a quick verbal or written quiz, students try to recall the general usage of the different punctuation marks.

TIP 19: WRITING WITH CONFIDENCE

In general, students often prefer to talk rather than write. However, one basic method that helps to give them confidence in their writing is to ask them to write on the board as a team effort each team taking it in turns to add a sentence according to the written task requirements.

Task 1: to convey information

- In a given time, students use the internet to gather information about a chosen topic. Students make written notes as they search. In teams or in pairs, students write a paragraph incorporating the information gathered.

- Students write down 5 instructions for making something e.g. a model aeroplane, a cake, a piece of furniture. Students swap papers or the opposing team tries to name the object that is being made.

Task 2: to clarify meaning

- Students complete **worksheet 24**. Two teams compete to think of more words that sound the same but are spelt differently and have a different meaning.

- Two teams compete to think of words that have more than one meaning e.g. dry: dry not wet, a dry sense of humour. One team provides the different meanings; the other team names the word. Students select from the examples given to write a paragraph or more that uses a term in a specific way e.g. a paragraph that describes how something demonstrated his/her 'dry' sense of humour.

- The teacher extracts confusing statements from the students' writing and writes them on the board. Teams compete to 'correct' and clarify the examples.

- Students write a paragraph describing an activity. The final sentence only contains the vital information that specifies the activity. In pairs, students share their paragraphs, providing only the first letters of the final sentence e.g. She stepped cautiously into the water. She could hear a voice calling to her. She walked in up to her waist … (final sentence S___ w____ l____ t___ s___. (She was learning to swim).

Task 3: responding to a short passage or pictures

- Students look at different pictures or texts critically. Students specify their purpose (why they are writing e.g. to describe their picture) format (the form of their writing e.g. critique, short newspaper/magazine article, letter, report) and audience (e.g. schoolchildren, artists, parents). They write a critique of the picture or text for the judges of a photographic/writing competition. Class critiques are compared to find the most favoured picture(s)/texts.

TIP 20: PAINLESS PARAGRAPHS

- Students underline the most important words in the question and make a plan using each underlined word as a heading

- The teacher suggests an essay format: e.g.
  paragraph 1 answers the question briefly
  paragraph 2, 3 etc. describe more fully each point made in the introductory paragraph
  the final paragraph summarizes

- Students write an essay without guidance. Afterwards, the students or teacher chooses the best example as a model for their next essay.

  e.g., writing essays: for and against
- Suggest an essay format: e.g.
  paragraph 1 presents a summary of arguments for and against a particular point of view regarding the subject.
  paragraph 2 gives reasons for in more detail
  paragraph 3 gives reasons against in more detail
  paragraph 4 decides which argument 'wins'

- Students to take one point of view and provide three or more supportive facts that support this view. Each fact is amplified in a separate paragraph. A final paragraph gives support for why the opposite point of view has not been taken.

- Students make a list of all the supporting facts for or against a subject. In separate paragraphs, they expand one fact and describe how the fact supports a particular point of view and does not support the other. Students summarize with the most effectively supporting facts.

- Students take one point and write a paragraph supporting it. Students write a second paragraph offering an opposing view and supporting it, if possible, or explaining why the view is unsupported. A third paragraph supports one of the views and explains why it is preferable to the other.

END

WORKSHEET 1 What do you need most? Name of student(s): _____

1. In rank order, numbering 1 to 5, what do you need most? (That is, if you need to practise speaking most, you will write the number 1 next to 'Speaking'. If the next most important item you need to practise is grammar, you will write number 2 next to 'Grammar' and continue.)

Speaking _____

Listening_____

Reading_____

Writing_____

Grammar_____

2. Tick the areas you need most:

- vocabulary _____
- understanding the differences between facts, ideas and opinions _____
- understanding social registers and styles _____
- using different ways to restrict language _____
- making inferences _____
- using a variety of grammatical structures _____

In Speaking being able to:
- influence the direction of conversation _____
- use suitable pronunciation and stress patterns _____
- take part in role play, interviews, telephone conversations, paired or group discussions and debates _____
- answer questions on specific topics _____
- show a sense of audience _____

In Listening being able to:
- understand short extracts: dialogues, announcements, conversations ... ___
- identify attitudes _____
- draw conclusions _____

In Reading be able to:
- skim-/gist-read texts such as advertisements, instructions. _____
- understand more detailed comprehension texts such as a report, newspaper ... _____.
- transfer information _____
- summarise _____
- write approximately 100-150 or 150 - 200 in response to pictures or prompts _____

In Writing be able to: use appropriate paragraphing, punctuation and spelling _____

WORKSHEET 2 Introduce yourself (writing)

Name of student: _____

Write as much as you can, introducing yourself to your teacher. Include topics such as your family, your hobbies, your likes and dislikes, your future plans, and write a story about something special that happened to you in the past. Finish with describing what you find easy and difficult about English.

_____

_____

_____

_____

_____

_____

_____

_____

_____

_____

_____

_____

_____

_____

Examples of students' answers to **WORKSHEET 2**

STUDENT 1.

My name Josef. I come from London. I has two brothers and one sister. My father is shop assistant. My mother is cleaner in school. I am student. I listen music and go in town with my friends. I like sport. I not like homework. Future I will go university. I will be a teacher sport. When I is 4, I run into street and my arm broken. Speak English is easy, write in English is difficult.

STUDENT 2.

Hello teacher. My name is Anna and I live in London with my mother, my father and my two sisters. My parents work at the garage on the corner of my street. My father is mechanic and my mother is the secretary. I go to school every day except Saturdays and Sundays. On the mornings I deliver papers. I like ride my bicycle to town. I don't like making housework and I hate getting up early to do the paper round. Also, my mother makes me make too much housework. In the future I hope to go to university and become an engineer. My Dad wanted to be an engineer but his Mum and Dad were too poor pay fees in America. They lived in America long time. Speaking and writing in English is easy. I contemplate grammar is difficult.

STUDENT 3

Hi teacher. You call me Chuck. My pals call me Chuck. My Ma and Pa call me Charles but me and my pals say Charles is silly name. My name is Chuck, okay?

My family. My family are big. I have three sisters and two brothers. I don't have no hobbies. I like mucking about with my pals. I don't like the boy next door. He is too bored. Maybe I go away at home one day. English speaking is easy. I hate writing. .

STUDENT 4

Can one really understand oneself fully enough to be able to write a comprehensive account of one's self? What does 'self' mean? Am I real, or a figment of my imagination? Is my understanding of myself valid? Should one ever attempt to describe one's personality, likes and dislikes or habits? Such a description can only be wholly successful if completed by someone who is very well acquainted with you as an individual.

WORKSHEET 3 Can you correct these errors?

e.g. I have *much* friends. **I have many friends.**

1. *My name Carlos.* _____

2. *My father is manager.* _____

3. *My family are big.* _____

4. *I has two brothers.* _____

5. *I like ride my horse.* _____

6. *I listen music.* _____

7. *On the mornings I deliver papers.* _____

8. *I make the housework* _____

9. *I not like homework.* _____

10. *I will be a teacher sport.* _____

11. *Parents were too poor pay for study* _____

12. *I don't like it. It is too bored.* _____

13. *In the past, when I is 4, I run.* _____

14. *I my arm broken* _____

15. *They lived in Wales long time.* _____

16. *Speak English is easy.* _____

17. *I contemplate grammar is difficult.* _____

18. *Call me Bill, okay?* _____

WORKSHEET 4 Can you correct these common errors?

e.g. I have *much* friends. **I have many friends.**

1. How *many* sugar have you? _____

2. There are *less* people on the train now. _____

3. There is *fewer* trouble at matches now. _____

4. Please let me *to* lend you … _____

5. I look forward to *see* you. _____

6. I like *apple*. _____

7. The man *do* not understand. _____

8. I haven't *some* books. _____

9. I no have no money. _____

10. I hope *coming* … _____

11. I have seen *never* … _____

12. She *like* it. _____

13. I came at home. _____

14. I will call to you on your mobile. _____

15. I am busy most of the times. _____

16. Regards to your all friends. _____

17. I look forward to hear from you. _____

18. You are well come. _____

19. Have you any thing for me? _____

20. The courses is free. _____

WORKSHEET 5 Vocabulary: Education

A: Group the words or phrases according to the topic:

Words to choose from: *curriculum, to revise, timetable, to take an exam, employee, to accept a position, to go for an interview, to apply for a job, news flash, media, broadcast, journalist, headlines, pandemic, general practitioner, epidemic, resuscitate, remedy, to take a trip, to go on an expedition, to go on an excursion, to go sightseeing, to globetrot, vacation, half-term holiday, a sabbatical, skiing*

e.g. *Education*: **curriculum, to revise**

Education: _____

Work: _____

_____

Current affairs: _____

Health and welfare: _____

Travel: _____

Holidays: _____

B: Match the word with its meaning:

e.g. doctor **general practitioner**

1. A medicine to cure a disease or pain that is not very serious_____

2. A large number of an infectious disease occurring at the same time _____

3. The subjects that are taught by a school _____

4. To make someone breathe again _____

5. Illness of disease that affects the population of a large area _____

6. A period when someone, probably at university, stops doing their usual work in order to

   study or travel _____

7. To travel to many different countries _____

WORKSHEET 6 Name the part of speech

Choose from:

a noun (such as 'table')

an article (such as 'a' or 'the')

a conjunction (such as 'and' in 'He walked into the room and he closed the door.')

an auxiliary verb (such as 'have' in 'have done')

an interjection (such as Wow!)

a modal verb (such as 'may' in 'He 'may' be late.')

a preposition (such as 'to' in 'Go to the station.')

an adjective (such as 'beautiful')

a verb (such as 'write' in 'They write letters every day.')

an adverb (such as 'quickly' in 'She spoke quickly.')

e.g. specifies a thing or person **a noun**

1. a word of action, a 'doing' word _____

2. a word that shows whether a noun is a particular or general thing _____

3. an additional verb to show tense, person or mood _____

4. adds meaning to a noun _____

5. an exclamation _____

6. an additional verb to express possibility, permission or intension _____

7. a word connecting nouns, pronouns or gerund _____

8. a word that joins phrases and clauses _____

9. adds meaning to a verb _____

Worksheet 7 Place the verb tenses with the description: THE PRESENT

Choose from:

The present simple, e.g. I write, the present perfect, e.g. I 'have written', the present perfect continuous, e.g. I have been writing, the present continuous, e.g. I am writing

e.g. **The present simple e.g. I write** is used to describe:

- a routine habit or repeated action
- a general truth or fact, .
- a permanent situation,
- in a time clause after: when, as soon as, if, until
- to describe future timetables

_____ is used to describe:

- a temporary situation
- an action happening now
- future arrangements
- annoying habits

_____ is used to describe:

- An action or situation which started in the past and finished recently
- A series of repeated actions in the pas t which may continue into the present
- When we want to focus on the result of the action
- When we want to focus on the number of times the action occurred
- The action itself (even when completed) in the past e.g. I have met many famous people.

_____ is used:

- when we want to focus on the action itself
- when we want to focus on the duration of the action

Worksheet 8 Place the verb tenses with the description: PAST AND FUTURE

Choose from:

the past continuous, e.g. I was writing, going to, the past perfect, e.g. 'I had written', will, the past simple, e.g. I wrote

e.g. **The past simple e.g. I wrote** is used to describe:

- A sequence of events in the past
- An action that interrupts another
- An action or situation in the past where the exact time is given

_____ is used to describe:

- background information to a narrative
- An action which is interrupted by another

'_____' is used when a decision is made at the time of speaking e.g. If he is not here in ten

minutes, I _____ not wait for him.

'_____' is used when we know what we are _____ do beforehand e.g. when we

make plans, make decisions or express firm intentions e.g. I _____ finish this before

I go home tonight.

_____ is used to describe:
- Something that happened in the past before something else in the past
- What had happened to cause a result in the past. e.g. the car crashed. The driver had fallen asleep.

_____ is used:

- When we want to focus on the action itself before something else that happened in the past
- When we want to focus on the duration of the action before something else that happened in the past

Worksheet 9 EDITING GUIDE

1. article? a? the? no article? (countable or uncountable?)
    e.g. a book (we don't know which one)
      the book on the table (we know which one – the one on the table)
      Books are found in most homes. (We don't know how many –'books' has a general meaning – 'books everywhere')

2. verb? verb form? tense?
is the verb missing? e.g. a sentence = subject + verb e.g. The boy ran.
verb form? e.g. He has pass exam. WRONG
        e.g. He has passed his exam. RIGHT
tense? e.g. We go to school (present simple – we do it everyday, often)
We are going to school (present continuous – we are doing it NOW or we have decided to do it in the future.)
They have gone to catch the bus for school – present perfect = happens in the past just before the present
We were going to school when the bus arrived = past continuous - happens in the past before something else in the past, or when interrupted by something else in the past.

3. participle correct? past participle e.g. It is close. WRONG It is closed. RIGHT.
           present participle e.g. He is run. WRONG He is running. RIGHT

4. active? e.g. It is closed. Passive? It was closed by the last student.

5. preposition? preposition missing? He went the shops. WRONG He went to the shops RIGHT.
correct preposition? He sat over the chair WRONG He sat on the chair RIGHT.
preposition not needed? e.g. He repaired up the chair. WRONG He repaired the chair. RIGHT.

6. spelling? Is the word spelt correctly? (use a dictionary or the wordcheck on your computer)
singular (book) or plural (books) ?

7. punctuation? e.g. capital letter? for a name e.g. 'Jill' or at the beginning of a sentence? end of a sentence? – full stop?

8. conjunction? (joins sentences – no capital) e.g. He worked hard because he wanted to pass his exams.
Conjunction missing? He bought fish chips WRONG He bought fish and chips RIGHT

9. wrong part of speech? a noun? (a thing or a person e.g. a boy), a verb? (a doing word – e.g. to run), an adjective? (describing word) e.g. the big boy, an adverb? (describes an action e,g, He ran quickly)

10. missing or too many letter(s) or word(s)? She knocked the door. WRONG She knocked at the door. RIGHT
a word or words not needed? or more words are needed to make sense or to make a complete sentence? e.g. A lady who disagrees. WRONG A lady, who disagrees, spoke against the suggestion. RIGHT.

Using the Editing Guide
Using this editing Guide, correct the following mistakes:
e.g. There is book on the table. Whose is it? (error 1) <u>There is **a** book on the table.</u>

1. See the filled glass on the table? Please give me glass now. (error 1) See the filled glass

   on the table? _____

2. She has pass her exam. (error 2) _____

3. Yesterday I go out. (error 2) _____

4. They was go to the bus stop when the car stopping in front of them. (error 2)

   _____

5. The shop is close (error 3) _____

6. The boy was closed by the door. (error 4) _____

7. She went at the door and opened it. (error 5) _____

8. I will phone to you tonight. (error 5) _____

9. I bought ten apple today (error 6). _____

10. She spoke to jane yesterday. (error 7) _____

11. He came early prepared the meal for me. (error 8)

    _____

12. She picked up the largely pen and wrote with it. (error 9)

    _____

13. I forgot to write my (error 10) _____

14. I will go to Cambridge tomorrow. (error 7) _____

Worksheet 10 PRONUNCIATION CHART

Consonants:
p as in pad
b as in bud
t as in top
d as in dot
k as in cat, (ache, pack, park, school, queen)
g as in go
ch as in church, (itch)
j as in judge, (giant)
m as in mat, (lamb)
n as in nun, (knife, pneumonia)
ng as in wing, (hunger)
l as in letter, (angle, funnel)
f as in fan, (photo, tough, laugh)
v as in vat
th as in teeth
TH as in feather
sh as in shop (assure, station, initial, sure)
zh measure
r as in rat (wrong)
h as in hat (who)
w as in word (wheel, quick, once)
ks as in box, (socks, books)
y as in yo-yo, (unit, civilian, million)
s as in sack, (miss, horse, city, price)
z as in zero, (busy, sneeze, dogs, nose)

vowels:
I as in feet, (me, tea, key, funny, piece)
i as in kid (physics)
e as in bed (head, said)
a as in bat
ar as in card, (bath, half)
o as in dot, (watch, cough)
or as in fort (although, saw, audience, caught, bought)
oo as in took, (full)

ooo as in food, (to, you, rude, new, sue, who, queue)
u as in cup, (one, enough, dozen, money)
er as in bird, (fern, burn, rehearsal)
ə as in lemon, (sugar, teacher, doctor, minus)

diphthongs:
ei as in rain, (baby, make, may, eight)
ə o as in coast, (open, snow, cope, dough)
ɑ i as in kite. (lion. light, dry, height)
ao as in cow (out, bough, doubt)
oI as in coil (toy, buoy)
I ə as in ear, (cheer, pier, weird)
eə as in bear, (air, care, mayor)
ooo ə as in fuel, (music)

35

Worksheet 11 Pronunciation:
Match these words with an example: a<u>ch</u>e, giant, <u>ph</u>oto, lau<u>gh,</u> sta<u>ti</u>on, ini<u>ti</u>al, <u>s</u>ure, <u>qu</u>ick,<u> once,</u> civi<u>li</u>an, hor<u>se,</u> <u>c</u>ity, pri<u>ce</u>, bu<u>sy</u>, do<u>gs</u>, no<u>se</u>, m<u>e</u>, k<u>ey</u>, p<u>ie</u>ce,<u> a</u>lthough, <u>s</u>aw, c<u>au</u>ght, b<u>ou</u>ght, t<u>o,</u> r<u>u</u>de, wh<u>o,</u> <u>queue,</u> en<u>ough</u>, m<u>o</u>ney, f<u>ern</u>
e.g. pa<u>ck</u> a<u>ch</u>e

1. <u>f</u>ace _____

2. <u>sh</u>one _____

3. <u>f</u>unny _____

4. m<u>e</u> _____

5. <u>w</u>inter _____

6. <u>y</u>es _____

7. <u>j</u>ar _____

8. <u>s</u>o _____

9. <u>z</u>ed _____

10. m<u>o</u>re _____

11. <u>w</u>on _____

12. <u>z</u>ip _____

13. f<u>ee</u> _____

14. <u>or</u> _____

15. p<u>u</u>p _____

16. <u>z</u>one _____

17. <u>sh</u>ip _____

18. f<u>or</u> _____

19. c<u>u</u>t _____

20. s<u>ir</u> _____

Worksheet 12 Stress: write the words next to the stress pattern described.
e.g., *Words of two syllables:*
stress on the first syllable (nouns) PROduce, **CONtract, CONduct REsearch** (also: FINish LITter MIRror MODel OFfer HONour TURkish …)

Choose from: conTRACT ADvertising reSEARCH BEAUtiful emPLOYment sucCESsful referEE DIFficulty conDUCT conVENience catAStrophy beneFIcial DANGerous exPLOratory deBILitative amBIguously princiPALity JapanESE eduCAtional nondeDUCtible debiliTAtion finalizAtion qualifiCAtions deMOcracy infinitESimal REPutable EXercises adHERence noncompleMENTary HANDicap

stress on the second syllable (verbs) proDUCE,_____

(prefixes (con- pro- il- …) and suffixes (-ion ly –ful -fully …) are not usually stressed

words of three syllabies:

stress on the first syllable: BENefit,_____

stress on the second syllable: connivance _____

stress on the third syllable: employee _____

words of four syllables:

stress on the first syllable: QUESTionable_____

stress on the second syllable: conVIVial_____

stress on the third syllable: eduCAtion_____

stress on the fourth syllable: interviewEE

words of five syllables:

stress on the second syllable: coORdinator _____

stress on the third syllable: eleMENtary _____

stress on the fourth syllable: communiCAtion _____

words of six or more syllables:

stress on the fourth syllable idioSYNcrasy _____

Worksheet 13 Facts Quiz: Business

Student A holds this answer sheet. Student A reads out the statement. Student B tries to guess the right answer.

Topic: Business:

1. The city in the UK known for the invention of the bicycle and a large car industry is a)

London **b) Coventry** c) Bristol

2. Creating a product or service, advertising it, and selling it is called a) selling b) advertizing **c)**

marketing

3. Short, memorable catchphrases used in advertizing are called a) proverbs **b) slogans** c) slang

4) Companies sometimes advertize through a) networking **b) public relations (PR)** c) meetings

5) The currency of the UK is **a) the pound** b) the euro c) the yen

6) Money that is owed is called the a) the deficit **b) debt** c) demand

7) Decrease of something through wear tear old age is called a) deficit b) devaluation **c)**

depreciation

8) money needed to pay for something is called **a) finance** b) payment c) feasibility

9) The rate charged for the use of money that is borrowed is called a) bonus **b) interest** c)

commission

10) a list of goods is called **a) an inventory** b) an invoice c) a compendium

Worksheet 14 Facts Quiz: Education

Student A holds this answer sheet. Student A reads out the statement. Student B tries to guess the right answer.

Education: Select the right answers:

1. In the UK:

Children under **a) 5** b) 4 c) 6 attend a nursery

Children aged a) 4-12 **b) 5 – 11** c) 6-13 attend a primary or junior school

Children a) 13-17 **b) 11-16 c) 12-18** attend a secondary school

2. Children stay in school for the longest time in:

a) The United Kingdom b) **Norway** c) Australia

3. Children stay in school for the least time in:

a) Mali b) Bulgaria c) Fiji

4. The country in which children read the most novels is

a) The United Kingdom b) The United States of America **c) New Zealand**

5. In the United Kingdom all children between a) 4 and 12 **b) 5 and 16** c) 5 and 18 must be in

full time education.

6. a) London **b) Milton Keynes** c) Oxford is the headquarters of the Open University.

7. The first serious intelligence tests were conducted in

a) 1905 b) 1850 c) 1940

8. Intelligence tests were first commissioned by the Government of

a) the UK b) Germany **c) France**

9. The average IQ (intelligence quotient) of today's tests is:

a) 50 **b) 100** c) 120

Worksheet 15 Facts Quiz: Health and Welfare

Student A holds this answer sheet. Student A reads out the statement. Student B tries to guess the right answer.

<u>Health and welfare:</u>

1. In the UK doctors are called a) home doctors b) medical staff **<u>c) general practitioners</u>**

2. In the UK medical needs are provided by the a) hospitals b) doctors **<u>c) NHS</u>**

3. NHS stands for **<u>a) the National Health Service</u>** b) the National Horticultural Society c) the

Northern Healing Society

4. The brain uses **<u>a) 20%</u>** b) 10% c) 5% of all the oxygen we breathe.

5. . Ancient Egyptian doctors used a) leaves b) cloths **<u>c) adhesive plasters</u>** on wounds

6. The body's largest organ is a) the liver **<u>b) the skin</u>** c) the heart

7. About a) 50% b) 30% **<u>c) 14%</u>** of the air is changed in our lungs with each breath.

8. Nerve impulses from the brain can travel as fast as a) 240km (150 mph) b) **<u>290 km/h (180 mph)</u>** c 120km/h(75 mph)

9. In the Western world, most people die of **<u>a) heart disease</u>** b) lung disease c) cancer

10. Compared with coffee, tea contains **<u>a) more</u>** b) less c) the same amount of caffeine.

Worksheet 16 Facts Quiz: Holidays

Student A holds this answer sheet. Student A reads out the statement. Student B tries to guess the right answer.

Holidays:

1. Britain's biggest theme part is a) Cadbury's World **b) Alton Towers** c) Legoland

2. Nowadays people can stay in a hotel on King George Island a) the Arctic b) Africa **c)**

Antarctica

3. The ice cap of Antarctica contains a) 70 **b) 90** c) 89 per cent of the world's ice.

4. Ottawa was chosen as the capital of Canada a) because it is in the best position **b) to resolve a squabble for position by 4 other cities** c) because it was the largest city

5. Mexico city is slowly sinking because **a) it is built on a reservoir of water** b) it is built on poor soil c) it is in an earthquake area

6. The capital city of Australia is named after the aboriginal word canberry which means a a) dwelling place b) water hole **c) meeting place**

7. The capital of Hungary, Budapest is named **a) after 2 cities joined together** b) a god-like statue c) a river

8. Tehran, the capital of Iran means a) city b) hill **c) plain**

9. The flag for Canada has a) a mountain **b) a leaf** c) a flower in the centre

10. The flag for Switzerland has a) a red cross b) **a white cross** c) a green cross in the centre.

Worksheet 17 Facts Quiz: Travel

Student A holds this answer sheet. Student A reads out the statement. Student B tries to guess the right answer.

Travel: (Great Britain):

1. Great Britain consists of two kingdoms: England and a) Wales b) **Scotland** c) Ireland

2. Great Britain also contains the principality of a) **Wales** b) Scotland c) Ireland

3. a) Southern Island c) **Northern Ireland** is another part of the United Kingdom of Great Britain.

4. a) Great Britain b) **Northern Island** c) **Southern Ireland** are part of the European Union (EU)

5. The capital of England is a) Dublin b) **London** c) Edinburgh.

6. The official home of the monarch, Queen Elizabeth the 2nd I a) **Buckingham Palace** b) Kensington Palace c) Hampton Court

7. The British Prime Minister lives in London at a) 10 Mayfair b) **10 Downing St.** c) 10 Baker St.

8. Emily Bronte who wrote *Jane Eyre* grew up in the village of a) Hayward **b) Hawarth West Yorkshire** c) Heathcliff East Yorkshire

9. Stonehenge consists of a circle of large stones on a) Thames Embankment in London b) the Moors in Yorkshire **c) Salisbury Plain in Wiltshire**

10. Oast houses in the countryside in Kent and East Sussex were once used to dry the a) grass b) barley **c) hops** collected to make beer

Worksheet 18 Vocabulary: Ideas

Fill the gaps with appropriate words from this list:

adapt / adjust / adjustments / aim / alter / alterations / amend / amendments / change / changes /

design / goal / idea / improve / improvements / intention / modifications / modify / object /

objective / plan / project / proposal / proposition / purpose / recommendation / reorganize /

reshape / revamp / revise / revisions / scheme / suggestion / tailor / target / vary

e.g. 1. I have a **plan/ proposal** …

2. I think there is a flaw in the _____.

3. My/our _____ would be to cater for all needs.

4. May I make a _____?

5. My/Our _____ would be to …

6. If we _____ the weaknesses in our plan …

7. If I were in charge, I would_____ (something)

by –ing …

8. I think they should _____

(something) to suit/satisfy/ …

9. If you are considering making any _____,

these should only be put into place after all interested parties have been consulted.

10. The o_____ of the exercise is to make sure no one has any reason to o____ to our s_____.

Worksheet 19 Register

1. Group some of the following words into very informal, informal, formal and very formal words: *choose from:* **(to like)**: *to be fond of, to be attached to, to have regard for, to think well of, to hold in esteem, admire, respect, be attracted to, fancy, find attractive, be keen on, be taken with, take a shine to, be into*

(to dislike): *dislike, hate, loathe, detest, abhor, despise, feel aversion towards, feel revulsion towards, feel hostile towards, be repelled by, be revolted by, not be able to bear/stand, be unable to stomach, find intolerable, shudder at, recoil from, shrink from*

e.g. very informal: to fancy; informal: to be fond of ...; formal: to think well of ...; very formal: to have regard for ...;

very informal:

_____

informal:

_____

formal:

_____

very formal:

_____

2. Match the sentences with the descriptions of types of vocabulary:

Suggested types of vocabulary: Academic (used in theses at universities); Colloquial (everyday words or phrases used mainly in speaking rather than writing); Formal (used on a formal occasion or when speaking to someone we should respect); Informal (used in everyday conversation); Literary (used in literature more than in ordinary writing or speaking); Medical (used in medicine or the treatment of disease and injury); Old-fashioned (words that are still part of the language but are rarely used by the younger generation); Poetic (uses vocabulary that expresses deep feelings or uses graceful phrases/clauses); Plain (easy to understand); Slang (very informal words used between particular groups of people, words not normally used in ordinary conversation)

a. The methodology used to categorize holidays … _____
b. Where are you going for your vacation? _____
c. Holidays don't come cheap. _____
d. Do you know a great place to go for our hols? _____
e. I am advised that you represent a reputable tour company _____
f. Miss Maria Ward had the good luck to captivate the wealthy baron with the prospect of many charming holidays abroad. _____
g. I like holidays. _____
h. You will need a prescription for your travel sickness. _____
i. I'm really hacked off. We are not going on holiday after all _____
j. High on the hills for our holidays … _____

Worksheet 20 STYLE

Fill in the missing prepositions: *A description of different styles concerns ways in which words are selected and sentences and paragraphs are structured and combined __ express the author's ideas. It includes the way general feelings, attitudes and opinions are expressed and the effect __ the intended audience.*
e.g. Romantic (a late 18ᵗʰ and early 19ᵗʰ century style __ which feelings and wild natural beauty are most important); Academic (used in theses __ universities); Elaborate (complex, full __ detail, phrases/clauses are connected in a complex way); Formal (used __ a formal occasion); Informal (containing language that is used __ everyday conversation); Journalistic (gives facts, mentioning who, what, when, where, why and how __ articles __ a few well-chosen words); Literary (used __ literature more than in ordinary writing); Narrative (tells a story); Oratorical (includes long and formal words associated __ speeches); Plain (easy to understand, uncomplicated); Poetic (uses language that expresses deep feelings or contains graceful phrases/clauses)

Finish identifying the style:

e.g. I am much better for the beauty of soft meadows gently touched by sunlit raindrops.

Romantic

1. Authors disagree over the respective effectiveness of the medication._____

2. Are you okay? _____

3. May I ask if you are well? _____

4. Be kind to those less fortunate in health than you are, I implore you. _____

5. The doctor gave the medicine to the patient at 8 o'clock. _____

6. Health, one of the most important aspects of our existence, becomes more important to us as

    we are constantly caught up in the vicissitudes of daily living. _____

7. Anne's disposition was such that she could never even think of the consequences_____

8. It happened on a Sunday evening. The patient was walking towards his house when_____

9. Heavenly intervention healed the poor patient. He cried aloud. 'I live!' _____

10. I take a spoonful of medicine every night. _____

Worksheet 21 PUNCTUATION

Fill the gaps

. (a full stop):

- ends a sent____
- ends a short____ word e.g. Oct. (Oct____) unless it uses the last letter e.g. Dr (doctor)

... (3 full stops): mark words left ___ e.g. 'I said that ... in the future.'

, (a comma):

- sep_rates words, clauses or phrases e.g. She bought flour, tea and butter.
- marks off introductory words from the main part of a s_____ e.g. 'In spite of this, progress has been slow.'

; (a semi-colon):

- separates items in a list when they have commas bet_____ them e.g. Extras for his model include: windows, electrically operated; master switch; tinted glass; steel exhaust.
- separates cl__ses closely connected with each other e.g. Old customs have lingered on here: I have recently seen some maypole dancers.

: (a colon):

- introduce_s speech or a list e.g. He called: 'Come here' or e.g. The following will be sold: bookcases, books, desks.
- occasionally a colon separates statements w____ are contrasted e.g. Man proposes: God disposes

? (a question mark):

- is put at the end of a quest___ but not in reported (or 'indirect') speech. e.g. Shall we go? I asked if we should go.

! (an exclamation mark):

- is used after interjections and excla_____ e.g. Wait a minute! or Help!

' (an apostrophe):

- shows posses**s**___ e.g. this man's cap; those ladies' hats:
- to a singular no__ adds 's e.g. Jane, Jane's cap
- a singular plural noun end___ in 's' adds the apostrophe only e.g. boy, boys, boys'
- a plural no__ not ending in 's' adds 's e.g. women, women's rights
- a singular personal no__ ending in 's' adds 's e.g. James James's hat
- no apostrophe is used f__ 'yours' or 'theirs' e.g.'The car is theirs'
- when showing possession, no apos_____ is used in 'its' e.g. It returned to its base.
- common wo_ds use it to show missing letters e.g.,: hasn't. didn't, two o'clock, the winter of '99/-07

' ' or **" "** (inverted commas) are used to show actual wo_ds spoken or written

( ) (round brackets) sho_ inserted words e.g. 'Caesar (Mark Anthony's friend) was feared.'

[ ] (square bra_____s) show words that are quoted but are not part of a whole text already being quoted e.g. The main passage is: 'I agree that it [the treasure] was lost.'

—the dash:

- can be used in pairs inste_d of ( )
- can separate a summing up statement from items before it e.g. addition, subtraction, multiplication — all made up the maths programme.

-(the hyphen) links the words that make up a compound wo_d e.g. mother-in-law

46

Worksheet 22 SPELLING
Fill the gaps:
e.g. To get something is to rec**eive** something.

1. You need strong teeth to bit__

2. My friend call me on the phone today. She had phon____ me ten times yesterday.

3. No one is allowed to smoke inside any more. Smoking inside is ban____.

4. I will be mak____ a cake this afternoon.

5. I want to see the monk__ in the zoo.

6. The snow is a bit flak__ tonight.

7. The room was ful__ of people.

8. They were very helpfu__.

9. The train is at the sta____

10. He lives in a big man____

11. It was a bit of an ant__climax.

12. My mother went to the ant__natal clinic.

13. She is always very cau____ when she drives her father's car.

14. Is he awake? Is he cons____?

Worksheet 23 PUNCTUATION:
A. Match the punctuation mark with its function
e.g. ends a sentence: . (**a full stop**)

1. ends a sentence: _____

2. marks off introductory words from the main part of a sentence: _____

3. separates clauses closely connected with each other: _____

4. ends a shortened word e.g. Oct: _____

5. introduces speech or a list: _____

6. is put at the end of a question: _____

7. shows possession: _____

8. separates words, clauses or phrases: _____

9. show actual words spoken or written: _____

10. show inserted words: _____

B. Put in the apostrophes:
1. this mans cap
2. those ladies hats:
3. Janes cap
4. Two boys books
5. womens rights
6. Jamess hat
7. mother-in-laws house

Put in the punctuation:

1. Nov and Dec would be the best months.

2. The boy ran

3. The girl who was late came in the front door.

4. In spite of her nagging he did not lock the gate.

5. Look out she cried

phones

Worksheet 24 HOMONYMS:

      Match the words with their homonyms (words that sound the same but are spelt differently and have a different meaning)

Choose from:

heir bare fair flour hair way coarse made medal knew hour peace bee rode see whole stationary sun their principal nun they're scene mail passed too two waste rowed whether know weak fined aisle would right grate

e.g. air ____   our ____

be ____   past ____

bear ____   piece ____

course ____   principle ____

fare ____   road (2) _____

find ____   sea ____

flower ____   seen ____

great ____   son ____

hare ____   stationery ____

hole ____   there (2) _____

isle ____   to (2) _____

maid ____   waist ____

male ____   weather ____

meddle ____   week ____

new ____   weigh ____

no ____   wood ____

none ____   write ____

Worksheet 25 What are the missing prepositions? Copy for <u>STUDENT A</u>

STUDENT A

The travel industry is an essential part **of** a country's economy. It is closely associated **with** the tourist industry and involves all forms **of** transport including road, rail, sea and air. Many tourists benefit from looking **on** the internet **for** cheap package holidays that are all-inclusive. Many travel companies offer advice **on** how to prepare **for** your journey. **Before** leaving your home, for example, you should take reasonable precautions **to** prevent your house **from** being burgled while you are away **by** arranging a friend or neighbour **to** check your property regularly. A very popular destination **for** people in Europe is the Costa Blanca **in** Spain. It is a 2-hour flight **from** the UK. Alicante's main international airport is 10km southwest **of** the city and about 15 minutes **to** the centre **by** bus or taxi. If you can be flexible **about** when you visit, you can pick **up** a special deal which can be quite cheap.

STUDENT B

As a rule, the further __advance you buy your tickets, the cheaper it usually is – but you can also get good last-minute deals __the internet. Before travelling, you should make sure your passport has at least three months __run __the start __your journey. You will also need to get some currency __you go especially if your flight arrives __the weekend or late __the day __the banks have closed. You should make sure that your credit and debit cards are up-to-date and do not expire __your holiday. With regard __health, you might consider it wise __pack a small first aid kit containing such items as plasters, antiseptic cream and sun lotion. If you take prescription medicines, make sure you have enough __last you __the whole holiday. Depending __the type of journey you have planned, baggage allowance can be very restrictive, especially __the budget airlines which sometimes only allow one case __each person.

WORKSHEET 25 What are the missing prepositions? Copy for <u>STUDENT B</u>

STUDENT A

The travel industry is an essential part __ a country's economy. It is closely associated __the tourist industry and involves all forms __transport including road, rail, sea and air. Many tourists benefit from looking __the internet __cheap package holidays that are all-inclusive.

Many travel companies offer advice __how to prepare __your journey. __leaving your home, for example, you should take reasonable precautions __prevent your house __being burgled while you are away __arranging a friend or neighbour __check your property regularly.

A very popular destination __people in Europe is the Costa Blanca __Spain. It is a 2-hour flight __the UK. Alicante's main international airport is 10km southwest __the city and about 15 minutes __the centre __bus or taxi. If you can be flexible __when you visit, you can pick __a special deal which can be quite cheap.

STUDENT B

As a rule, the further **in** advance you buy your tickets, the cheaper it usually is – but you can also get good last-minute deals **on** the internet. Before travelling, you should make sure your passport has at least three months **to** run **from** the start **of** your journey. You will also need to get some currency **before** you go especially if your flight arrives **at** the weekend or late **in** the day **after** the banks have closed. You should make sure that your credit and debit cards are up-to-date and do not expire **during** your holiday. With regard **to** health, you might consider it wise **to** pack a small first aid kit containing such items as plasters, antiseptic cream and sun lotion. If you take prescription medicines, make sure you have enough **to** last you **for** the whole holiday.

Depending **on** the type of journey you have planned, baggage allowance can be very restrictive, especially **on** the budget airlines which sometimes only allow one case **for** each person.

SUGGESTED ANSWERS TO THE WORKSHEETS

3. *My name Carlos.* **My name is Carlos** *My father is manager.* **My father is a manager.** *My family are big.* **My family is big.** *I has two brothers.* **I have two brothers.** *I like ride my horse.* **I like riding my horse./I like to ride my horse.** *I listen music.* **I listen to music.** *On the mornings I deliver papers.* **In the mornings I deliver newspapers.** *I make the housework.* **I do the housework.** *I not like homework.* **I do not like homework.** *I will be a teacher sport.* **I will be a sports teacher. / I will be a teacher of sport.** *Parents were too poor pay fees.* **The parents were too poor to pay the fees.** *I don't like it. It is too bored.* **I don't like it. It is too boring.** *In the past, when I is 4, I run.* **In the past, when I was 4, I ran.** *I my arm broken.* **I broke my arm.** *They lived in Wales long time.* **They lived in Wales a long time ago / for a long time.** *Speak English is easy.* **Speaking English is easy.** *I contemplate grammar is difficult.* **I think grammar is difficult.** *Call me Bill, okay?* **I would prefer you to call me Bill, if that would be all right with you.**

4. 1. How *many* sugar have you? **How much sugar do you take? 2.** There are *less* people on the train now. **There are fewer people on the train now.** 3. There is *fewer* trouble at matches now. **There is less trouble at matches now.** 4. Please let me *to* lend you … **Please let me lend you … 5.** I look forward to *see* you. **I look forward to seeing you.** 6. I like *apple.* **I like apples. 7.** The man *do* not understand. **The man does not understand.** 8. I haven't *some* books. **I haven't any books.** 9. I no have no money. **I have no money. / I haven't any money.** 10. I hope *coming* … **I hope to come … 11.** I have seen *never* … **I have never seen … 12.** She *like* it. **She likes it.** 13. I came *at* home. **I came home.** 14. I will call *to* you on your mobile. **I will call you on your mobile. 15.** I am busy most of the *times.* **I am busy most of the time.** 16. Regards to *your all* friends. **Regards to all your friends.** 17. You are *well come.* **You are welcome.** 18. Have you *any thing* for me? **Have you anything for me? 19.** The courses *is* free. **The courses are free. 20.** Yesterday he *speak.* **Yesterday he spoke.**

5. A:*Education*: **curriculum, to revise, timetable, to take an exam** ; *Work*: **employee, job, responsibilities, to accept a position, to go for an interview, to apply for a job;** *Current affairs*: **news flash, the media, broadcast, journalist, headlines ;** *Health and welfare:* **pandemic, general practitioner, epidemic, resuscitate, remedy;** *Travel*: **to take a trip, to go on an expedition, to go on an excursion, to go sightseeing, to globetrot;** *Holidays*: **vacation, half-term holiday, a sabbatical, skiing; B:** 1. A medicine … **remedy.** 2. A large number of … **epidemic.** 3. The subjects … **curriculum.** 4. **resuscitate.** 5. Illness … **a pandemic.** 6. A period … **sabbatical.** 7. To travel …**globetrot.**

6. 1. verb 2. article 3. auxiliary verb 4. adjective 5. interjection 6. modal verb 7. preposition 8. conjunction 9. Adverb

7. present simple; present continuous; present perfect; present perfect continuous

8. past continuous; will; going to; past perfect ; past perfect continuous

9. 1. Sec the filled glass on the table? Please give me **the** glass now. 2. She has pass**ed** her exam. 3. Yesterday I **went** out. 4. They **were going** to the bus stop when the car **stopped** in front of them. 5. The shop is clos**ed**. 6. **The boy closed** the door. 7. She went **to** the door and opened it. 8. I will phone you tonight. 9. I bought ten apple**s** today. 10. She spoke to **J**ane yesterday. 11. He came early **and** prepared the meal for me. 12. She picked up the **large** pen and wrote with it. 13. I forgot to write my **name**. 14. I will go to **C**ambridge tomorrow.

11. 1. face <u>ph</u>oto 2. <u>sh</u>one ini<u>ti</u>al 3. <u>f</u>unny lau<u>gh</u> 4. <u>m</u>e <u>p</u>iece 4. <u>w</u>inter qui<u>ck</u> 5. <u>y</u>es civi<u>li</u>an 6. <u>j</u>ar <u>g</u>iant 7. <u>s</u>o <u>c</u>ity 8. <u>z</u>ed bu<u>sy</u> 9. <u>m</u>ore ca<u>ugh</u>t 10. <u>w</u>on <u>o</u>nce 11. <u>z</u>ip dog<u>s</u> 12. <u>f</u>ee <u>k</u>ey 13. <u>or</u> al<u>th</u>ough 14. <u>p</u>u<u>p</u> <u>m</u>oney 15. <u>z</u>one no<u>se</u> 16. <u>sh</u>ip <u>s</u>ure 17. <u>for</u> <u>s</u>aw 18. <u>c</u>ut en<u>ough</u> 19. <u>sir</u> <u>f</u>ern

12. stress on the second syllable (verbs) proDUCE, **conTRACT, conDUCT reSEARCH**
(prefixes (con- pro- il- …) and suffixes (-ion ly –ful -fully …) are not usually stressed
stress on the first syllable: BENefit, **HANDicap, BEAUtiful, DANGerous**
stress on the second syllable: conNIVance, **adHERence, emPLOYment, sucCESsful**
stress on the third syllable: emploYEE**, referEE JapanESE**
words of four syllables:
stress on the first syllable: QUESTionable, **DIFficulty, EXercises, REPutable, ADvertising**
stress on the second syllable: conVIVial, **conVENience, cataAStrophy , deMOcracy**
stress on the third syllable: eduCAtion, **beneFIcial**
stress on the fourth syllable: interviewEE
words of five syllables:
stress on the second syllable: coORdinator **exPLOratory deBIlitative amBIguously**
stress on the third syllable: eleMENtary **princiPALity eduCAtional nondeDUCTible**
stress on the fourth syllable: communiCAtion, **debiliTAtion, finalizAtion qualifiCAtions**
words of six or more syllables:
stress on the fourth syllable idioSYNcrasy **infinitESimal noncompleMENTary**

18. (Suggested answers)
1. I have a **plan/ proposal/ proposition/ suggestion/recommendation/ (an) idea.** Why not …
2. I think there is a flaw in the **design.**
3. My/our **project/scheme** would be to cater for all needs.
4. May I make a **recommendation**?
5. My/Our **aim/ intention/ objective/ object/ purpose/ goal/** would be to …
6. If we **target** the weaknesses in our plan …
7. If I were in charge, I would **change/ alter/ adjust/ adapt/ amend/ improve/ modify/ revise, reshape, revamp, reorganize, vary** (something) by –ing …
8. I think they should **tailor/ change/ alter/ adjust/ adapt/ amend/ improve/ modify/ revise, reshape, revamp, reorganize, vary** (something) to suit/satisfy/ …
9. If you are considering making any **amendments/changes/alterations/adjustments/ improvements/modifications/revisions,** these should only be put into place after all interested parties have been consulted.
10. The **object** of the exercise is to make sure no one has any reason to **object** to our **scheme**.

19. (suggested answers)

1. very informal: to fancy, to be keen on, to be taken with, to take a shine to, to be into, to hate
informal: to be fond of, to be attached to, to be attracted to, to find attractive, to dislike, to loathe, be revolted by, not able to bear/stand, be unable to stomach, shudder at, shrink from
formal: to think well of, to admire, to respect, to detest, to despise, , feel hostile towards, be repelled by, find intolerable, recoil from
very formal: to have regard for, to hold in esteem, to abhor, to feel aversion towards, to feel revulsion towards

2. a. The methodology used to categorize holidays …**1. Academic (formal)**
b. Where are you going for your vacation? **7. Old-fashioned (formal)**
c. Holidays don't come cheap. **2. Colloquial (informal)**
d. Do you know a great place to go for our hols? **4. Informal**
e. I am advised that you represent a reputable tour company **3. Formal**
f. Miss Maria Ward had the good luck to captivate the wealthy baron with the prospect of many charming holidays abroad. **5. Literary (formal)**
g. I like holidays. **9. Plain (informal)**
h. You will need a prescription for your travel sickness. **6 Medical (formal)**
i. I'm really hacked off. We are not going on holiday after all **10. Slang (informal)**
j. High on the hills for our holidays … **8. Poetic (informal)**

20. *Romantic (a late 18th and early 19th century style **in** which feelings and wild natural beauty are most important); Academic (used in theses **at** universities); Elaborate (complex, full **of** detail, phrases/clauses are connected in a complex way); Formal (used **on** a formal occasion); Informal (containing language that is used **in** everyday conversation); Journalistic (gives facts, mentioning who, what, when, where, why and how **in** articles **of** a few well-chosen words); Literary (used **in** literature more than in ordinary writing); Narrative (tells a story); Oratorical (includes long and formal words associated **with** speeches); Plain (easy to understand, uncomplicated); Poetic (uses language that expresses deep feelings or contains graceful phrases/clauses)*

1. Authors disagree over the respective effectiveness of the medication. **1. Academic**
2. Are you okay? **4. Informal**
3. May I ask if you are well? **3. Formal**
4. Be kind to those less fortunate in health that you are, I implore you. **8. Oratorical**
5. The doctor gave the medicine to the patient at 8 o'clock. **5. Journalistic**
6. Health, one of the most important aspects of our existence, becomes more important to us as we are constantly caught up in the vicissitudes of daily living. **2. Elaborate**
7. Anne's disposition was such that she could never even think of the consequences. **6. Literary**
8. It happened on a Sunday evening. The patient was walking towards his house when **7. Narrative**
9. Heavenly intervention healed the poor patient. He cried aloud. 'I live!' **10. Poetic**
10. I take a spoonful of medicine every night. **9. Plain**

21.

. (a full stop): ends a sentence ends a shortened word e.g. Oct. (October) unless it uses the last letter e.g. Dr (doctor)

… (3 full stops): mark words left out e.g. 'I said that … in the future.'

, (a comma):

- separates words, clauses or phrases e.g. She bought flour, tea and butter.
- marks off introductory words from the main part of a sentence e.g. 'In spite of this, progress has been slow.'

; (a semi-colon):

- separates items in a list when they have commas between them e.g. Extras for his model include: windows, electrically operated; master switch; tinted glass; steel exhaust.
- separates clauses closely connected with each other e.g. Old customs have lingered on here: I have recently seen some maypole dancers.

: (a colon):

- introduces speech or a list e.g. He called: 'Come here' or e.g. The following will be sold: bookcases, books, desks.
- occasionally a colon separates statements which are contrasted e.g. Man proposes: God disposes

? (a question mark):

- is put at the end of a question but not in reported (or 'indirect') speech. e.g. Shall we go? I asked if we should go.

! (an exclamation mark):

- is used after interjections and exclamations e.g. Wait a minute! or Help!

' (an apostrophe):

- shows possession e.g. this man's cap; those ladies' hats:
- to a singular noun adds 's e.g. Jane, Jane's cap
- a singular plural noun ending in 's' adds the apostrophe only e.g. boy, boys, boys'
- a plural noun not ending in 's' adds 's e.g. women, women's rights
- a singular personal noun ending in 's' adds 's e.g. James James's hat
- no apostrophe is used for 'yours' or 'theirs' e.g.'The car is theirs'
- when showing possession, no apostrophe is used in 'its' e.g. It returned to its base.
- common words use it to show missing letters e.g.,: hasn't. didn't, two o'clock, the winter of '99/-07

' ' or **" "** (inverted commas) are used to show actual words spoken or written

( ) (round brackets) show inserted words e.g. 'Caesar (Mark Anthony's friend) was feared.'

[ ] (square brackets) show words that are quoted but are not part of a whole text already being quoted e.g. The main passage is: 'I agree that it [the treasure] was lost.'

— the dash:

- can be used in pairs instead of ( )
- can separate a summing up statement from items before it e.g. addition, subtraction, multiplication — all made up the maths programme.

- (the hyphen) links the words that make up a compound word e.g. mother-in-law

22.

1. You need strong teeth to bit**e**
2. My friend call be on the phone today. She had phon**ed** me ten times yesterday.
3. No one is allowed to smoke inside any more. Smoking inside is ban**ned**.
4. I will be mak**ing** a cake this afternoon.
5. I want to see the monk**ey** in the zoo.
6. The snow is a bit flak**y** tonight.
7. The room was ful**l** of people.
8. They were very helpf**ul**.
9. The train is at the sta**tion**
10. He lives in a big man**sion**
11. It was a bit of an ant**i**climax.
12. My mother went to the ant**e**natal clinic.
13. She is always very cau**tious** when she drives her father's car.
14. Is he awake? Is he cons**cious**?

23

1. ends a sentence: **. (a full stop)**
2. marks off introductory words from the main part of a sentence: **, (a comma)**
3. separates clauses closely connected with each other: **; (a semi-colon)**
4. ends a shortened word e.g. Oct: **. (a full stop)**
5. introduces speech or a list: **: (a colon)**
6. is put at the end of a question: **? (a question mark)**
7. shows possession: **' (an apostrophe)**
8. separates words, clauses or phrases: **, (a comma)**
9. show actual words spoken or written: **'' or "" (inverted commas)**
10. show inserted words: **( ) (round brackets)**

B. Put in the apostrophes:
1. this man's cap
2. those ladies' hats:
3. Jane's cap
4. Two boys' books
5. women's rights
6. James's hat
7. mother-in-law's house

Put in the punctuation:
1. Nov. and Dec. would be the best months.
2. The boy ran.
3. The girl, who was late, came in the front door.
4. In spite of her nagging, he did not lock the gate.
5. "Look out!" she cried.

24. e.g. air **heir**

1. be **bee**

2. bear **bare**

3. course **coarse**

4. fare **fair**

5. find **fined**

6. flower **flour**

7. great **grate**

8. hare **hair**

9. hole **whole**

10. isle **aisle**

11. maid **made**

12. male **mail**

13. meddle **medal**

14. new **knew**

15. no **know**

16. none **nun**

17. our **hour**

18. past **passed**

19. piece **peace**

20. principle **principal**

21. road **rode** **rowed**

22. sea **see**

23. seen **scene**

24. son **sun**

25. stationery **stationary**

26. there **their** **they're**

27. to **too** **two**

28. waist **waste**

29. weather **whether**

30. week **weak**

31. weigh **way**

32. wood **would**

33. write **right**

END

For further information, contact RJWestwell (rjwestwell@hotmail.com; website: www.rjwestwell.co.uk)

Other books available from the author:

'Out of a Learner's Mouth' an amusing diary describing the trials and tribulations of learning Spanish as a beginner and a mature student (available from Burrows Bookshop, 9 High St. Passage, Ely, Cambs.CB7 4NB Tel: UK (01353) 669759 www.burrowsbookshop.co.uk).

'Teaching Language Learners' a book packed with ideas for teaching English as a Foreign Language (available from Cambridge International Book Centre, 44 Hills Rd., Cambridge, Cambs. UK CB2 1LA Tel: (01223) 365400).

"The Spelling Game" a book of over 90 spelling groups that can be taught while increasing vocabulary and the working memory in students.

'John, Dementia and Me' a semi-autobiographical novel on early-onset dementia (available from North Staffordshire Press Ltd.www.northstaffordshirepress.com).

3483578R00032

Printed in Great Britain
by Amazon.co.uk, Ltd.,
Marston Gate.